D0518897

THE BRIDE'S BOOK OF

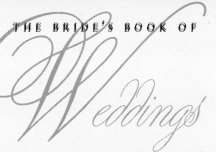

Weddings

Margaret Lannamann

Photographs by Laura Straus

ARIEL BOOKS

Andrews McMeel Publishing

Kansas City

www.andrewsmcmeel.com

Photographs © 1999 Laura Straus

ISBN: 0-7407-0058-8

Library of Congress Catalog Card Number: 99-60626

CONTENTS

INTRODUCTION

Whether your wedding celebration takes place on a quiet hilltop or you celebrate it with an elegant party with hundreds in attendance, this momentous day will be treasured and remembered forever. You want every detail to be perfect and every arrangement to go smoothly. Your marriage is a joyous occasion, the fulfillment of all

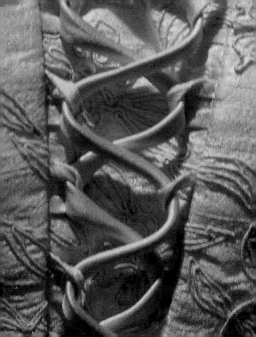

your hopes and dreams. It marks a milestone in your life, setting you on the threshold to a wonderful future of love and happiness.

Few occasions are as steeped in tradition as a wedding. To be sure, your marriage ceremony will reflect your tastes and those of the groom, but certain customs and conventions play a part in almost every wedding. Do you know why the bride wears white? How did the veil become a part of the bridal attire? Is it unlucky to marry in December? Why do many brides carry lilies? How did the custom of the groom carrying the bride over the threshold come to be? As you plan for your big day, use the wedding lore gathered in this book to make the occasion special.

You will also read about some modern, up-to-date touches you might like to use in your wedding, as well as suggestions for readings that will reflect the abiding love you share with your husband-to-be.

Enjoy this very exciting time in your life, and best wishes for the future!

THE PROPOSAL

*W*hether he pops the question on bended knee or whether the two of you make the decision together, the wedding proposal is one of the most excitingly romantic moments imaginable. Soon after it has taken place, however, all sorts of questions arise. How will you spread the news? What will your friends say? When will the ceremony take place?

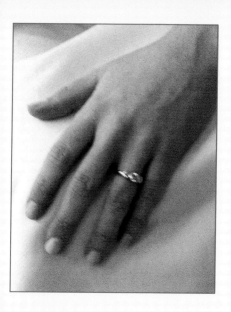

Before you get caught up in the countless details of planning for the future, relax and enjoy your happiness. Savor the moment and all that this important promise means in your life.

Two we are, and one we'll be,
If you'll consent to marry me.

—Anonymous

*I go about stammering, "I have
made that dear girl commit
herself, I have, I have," and
then I vault over the sofa
with exultation.*

—*Walter Bagehot*

*They gave each other a smile with
a future in it.*

—*Ring Lardner*

The fountains mingle with the
    river,
And the rivers mingle with the
    ocean;
The winds of heaven mix forever,
With a sweet emotion;
Nothing in the world is single,
All things by a law divine
In one another's being mingle—
Why not I with thine?

—*Percy Bysshe Shelley*

Raise me a dais of silk and down;
Hang it with vair and purple dyes;
Carve it in doves and pomegranates,
And peacocks with a hundred eyes;
Work it in gold and silver grapes,
In leaves and silver fleurs-de-lys;
Because the birthday of my life
Is come, my love is come to me.

—*Christina Rossetti*

*I*n early times, the engagement ring was the price the groom paid for the privilege of courting the bride; when she wore his ring, it was clear to all that she was his property. During the sixteenth and seventeenth centuries, the romantic side of the engagement came to the fore, and the circle of the engagement ring was viewed as a symbol of the lasting love the couple would share.

At about this time, "gimmal" rings became popular in Europe. The gimmal ring had two interlocking parts; one part was worn by the man and the other by the woman. When the marriage took place, the two rings were joined together and slipped on the bride's finger as the wedding ring.

The diamond became a popular choice for engagement rings in the mid-nineteenth century, when South African diamond mines began to produce enough diamonds to make purchasing such a ring feasible. Today, other types of precious stones are used as well, but the diamond is still the number-one favorite.

THE CEREMONY

*P*icking the date for the wedding can be a difficult decision. According to these old folk sayings, each month and each day of the week has particular advantages and disadvantages:

Marry when the year is new,
Always loving, kind, and true.

When February birds do mate
You may wed, nor dread your fate.

If you wed when March winds blow,
Joy and sorrow you'll both know.

Marry in April when you can,
Joy for maiden and for man.

Marry in the month of May,
You will surely rue the day.

Marry when June roses blow,
Over land and sea you'll go.

They who in July do wed
Must labor always for their bread.

Whoever wed in August be,
Many a change are sure to see.

Marry in September's shine,
Your living will be rich and fine.

If in October you do marry,
Love will come, but riches tarry.

If you wed in bleak November
Only joy will come, remember.

When December's snows fall fast,
Marry, and true love will last.

*W*hen Queen Victoria married Prince Albert in 1840, she looked breathtaking in a white satin gown with an eighteen-foot train, a white lace veil that hung down to her fingertips, and a garland of orange blossoms in her hair. Until that time, blue, gray, and silver were common colors for the wedding dress, but after Queen Victoria's marriage, brides began to imitate the Queen's white dress. Soon, the white wedding dress had become a tradition.

Many brides believe it is lucky to wear "something old, something new,

something borrowed, something blue." Something old represents continuity with the past, something new stands for the new life ahead. Something borrowed—often from a happily married woman—signifies good luck, and something blue symbolizes true love.

Wedding veils today are largely decorative and rarely cover the bride's face. At one time, however, the veil served an important function. Symbolizing purity, it protected the bride from the forces of evil—or, according to some, from the attentions of a jealous suitor.

Long ago, brides carried bouquets of garlic, grains, and herbs to keep evil spirits away and to ensure fertility and prosperity in marriage. Today's brides often choose more decorative flowers, many of which have symbolic value.

Aster	*Loyalty*
Baby's Breath	*Innocence*
Daffodil	*Respect*
Gardenia	*Joy*

Honeysuckle	*Faithful love*
Ivy	*Fidelity*
Lavender	*Sweet memories*
Lily	*Purity*
Lily of the Valley	*Sweetness*
Myrtle	*Love & constancy*

Orchid	*Fertility*
Rose	*Love*
Rosemary	*Fidelity*
Sunflower	*Happiness*
White Violet	*Opportunity*
Yarrow	*Married bliss*

*I love thee with a love I seemed to
   lose
With my lost saints—I love thee
   with the breath,
Smiles, tears, all of my life!—and,
   if God choose,
I shall but love thee better after
   death.*

*—Elizabeth
   Barrett Browning*

I am the word and you are the melody. I am the melody and you are the word.

—*Traditional Hindu mantra*

Now you will feel no rain,
for each of you will be a shelter to
     the other.
Now you will feel no cold,
for each of you will be warmth to
     the other.
Now there is no loneliness for you;
now there is no more loneliness.
Now you are two bodies,
but there is only one life before you.

Go now to your dwelling place,
to enter into your days together.
And may your days be good
and long on the earth.

—*Apache song*

Romance

I will make you brooches and toys for
    your delight
Of birdsong at morning and starshine
    at night
I will make a palace fit for you
    and me
Of green days in forests and blue days
    at sea.

I will make my kitchen and you
    shall keep your room
Where white flows the river and
    bright blows the broom,
And you shall wash your linen and
    keep your body white
In rainfall at morning and dewfall
    at night.

—⁓—

*And this shall be for music when no
one else is near,
The fine song for singing, the rare
song to hear!
That only I remember, that only you
admire,
Of the broad road that stretches and
the roadside fire.*

—*Robert Louis Stevenson*

Love is patient and kind; *love* is not jealous or boastful; it is not arrogant or rude. *Love* does not insist on its own way; it is not irritable or resentful; it does not rejoice at wrong, but rejoices in the right. *Love* bears all things, believes all things, hopes all things, endures all things. *Love* never ends. . . . So faith, hope, love abide, these three; but the greatest of these is love.

—*1 Corinthians 13:4-8, 13*

Long ago in ancient Egypt, the ring was used as a symbol of marriage, and it has been used as such throughout the world ever since. Whether it's a plain band or an elegant family heirloom, the wedding ring represents enduring love and serves as a visible—and beautiful—symbol of the wearer's married state.

Tradition dictates that the ring be worn on the fourth finger of the left hand. There are any number of explanations for this custom, the most likely being the ancient belief that the vein on this finger went straight to the heart.

It is sometimes customary to engrave the initials of the wedding couple and the date of the wedding on the inside of the wedding ring. Some choose to include a short verse as well. These words were taken from actual wedding rings:

The eye did find, ye heart did chuse,
The hand doth bind, til death doth loose.

If in thy love thou constant bee,
My heart shall never part from
  thee.

You and I will lovers be.

Thy consent is my content.

Of all the rest I love thee best.

During the marriage, the bride stands to the left of the groom. Long ago, this position freed the groom's right hand to wield his sword should the need arise.

Traditionally, the bride's father walked his daughter down the aisle, and when asked who it was that gave the woman in marriage, he would answer, "I do." Some brides in recent times have chosen to walk down the aisle escorted by both parents, who respond to the question with "We do."

THE
CELEBRATION

*C*elebrating the occasion of the wedding with a party goes back many centuries. In fact, the word *bridal* comes from the old English word *bridale,* which grew from a combination of the word *bride* and the word *ale.*

The celebration following a medieval wedding might last for a week—or even a month.

*T*he wedding cake has been part of the festivities from the earliest times. The ancient Greeks offered wheat and barley biscuits to the bride and groom, which were then crumbled over the bride's head to ensure fertility in the marriage. In the Middle Ages, these biscuits evolved into sweet buns, which the wedding guests would pile together at the wedding celebration, creating a stack that was later frosted in order to hold it together.

Cutting the wedding cake has always been an important ritual. Since the cake is symbolic of the fruitfulness of the marriage, the bride must cut into the cake before anyone else to avoid another person's "cutting into" her ability to have children.

Today's wedding cake, often created in beautifully decorated tiers, serves as a decorative centerpiece for the wedding reception. As the bride and groom feed each other the first bite, they are symbolizing the nurturing and love they will share in the coming years.

Sometimes young guests at the wedding are given a piece of the wedding cake to take home to put under their pillows, in

the hope that they will dream of the person whom they will someday marry.

*T*he tradition of throwing the bridal bouquet has its roots in ancient custom. Because the bride was viewed as particularly lucky on her wedding day, guests would tear at her clothing in order to take something away as a good luck token. To keep the mob happy, a bride would toss her bouquet—and sometimes her garter—to the assembled guests. In modern times, the woman who catches the bouquet is believed to be the next to marry.

The offering of toasts has long been a traditional part of most wedding celebrations, giving guests the opportunity to honor the wedding couple.

God, the best maker of all
marriages,
Combine your hearts in one.
*　　　—William Shakespeare*

Love, be true to her; Life, be dear to
    her;
Health, stay close to her; Joy, draw near
    to her.
Fortune, find what you can do for her,
Search your treasure-house through
    for her,
Follow her footsteps the wide world
    over,
And keep her husband always her lover.

           —Old English toast

*May your hands be forever clasped
in friendship and your hearts
joined forever in love.*

—*Anonymous*

*I*n old England, wedding guests showered newlyweds with nuts, shells, and even pieces of sod when the celebration was over. Rice, a symbol of fertility, has been thrown at weddings for centuries. Today's environmentally conscious newlyweds often substitute rose petals or birdseed for rice, because birds might be harmed by eating rice left on the ground; still others choose to be showered by bubbles blown by the guests.

SPECIAL
TOUCHES

*I*f you have access to some heirloom family lace, you might consider having it incorporated into your wedding dress or veil. Also, if your mother's wedding dress is available but not in shape for you to wear, consider using some of the fabric in your own dress or going-away outfit. ❧

At some point during the ceremony, stand facing the guests. 🖤

During the ceremony, hand a single rose to your mother and the mother of the groom. 🖤

Save some of the candles from the ceremony and light them during another special family occasion, such as your first anniversary or the birth of your first child. 🖤

Put a disposable camera on each table at the reception. Tell guests to snap photos of their group and leave the camera behind for processing. ❦

As small mementos or favors when the season permits, give flower bulbs to the guests, which they can plant in memory of your wedding day. ❦

SUPERSTITIONS

The custom of ringing bells after a wedding dates back to early times when noise was thought to ward off evil spirits.

If couples save a piece of their wedding cake, freeze it, and eat it on their first anniversary, good luck will shine on their marriage.

Passing a crumb of the wedding cake through the wedding ring means the marriage will endure.

If the bride cries before the wedding, she will have fewer tears after.

The bride should avoid seeing herself in a mirror by candlelight before the ceremony.

If the groom sees his bride wearing her wedding dress before the ceremony, it brings bad luck.

A dime in the bride's shoe brings prosperity to the married couple.

In order to ward off evil spirits, the bride should step out of her house with her right foot first instead of her left.

If the ring is dropped during the wedding ceremony, bad luck may follow.

In early times, the groom carried his bride across the threshold to avoid the evil spirits who were believed to haunt the doorway.

It means good luck if a bride sees a dove, a lamb, a spider, or a toad on her way to her wedding.

If a bride adds a last stitch to her wedding dress just as she is about to leave for the ceremony, it will bring good luck.

EVER AFTER

What woman, however old, has not the bridal favours and raiment stowed away, and packed in lavender, in the inmost cupboards of her heart.

—*William Makepeace Thackeray*

*A successful marriage requires
falling in love many times,
always with the same person.*
—*Mignon McLaughlin*

*Marriage is sought and kept alive
by a deep yearning to know
another and be known by
another.*
—*John Pierrakos*

Grow old along with me!
The best is yet to be,
The last of life, for which the first
was made . . .

—*Robert Browning*

SPECIAL THANKS TO:

ABIGAIL & AARON ASHER
ALEXANDRA DIAMOND
JEFFREY FUISZ
DIANA REEVE
THE SMITHS, NY
R.K. BRIDAL, NY
JANE WILSON-MARQUIS BRIDAL, NY

THE TEXT OF THIS BOOK IS SET IN
PERPETUA BY MSPACE, KATONAH,
NEW YORK.

BOOK DESIGN BY
MAURA FADDEN ROSENTHAL